1945 Early Memories of

House climbs with the Windermere Gr.
totally ill-equipped, to the top of some of the highest mountains in the district - Wetherlam (my house), Fairfield and Scafell (the rivals) - we climbed them all. The war had just ended - evacuees returned home - my father was back from the forces and I started to help on the boats at Bowness, just weekends and holidays, as of course sons of boatmen were expected to do.

I continued working on the boats after leaving school but only part time. National Service took me away from the area for two years and on my return in 1954 I vowed never to move away again.

I became a boatman full time in 1960 and walking became a winter only activity. The summer was spent advising all and sundry to come and enjoy the beauty of the lake, nevertheless over the years I have managed to get to the top of most of the Lakeland fells.

However, time moves on, I am now a few years past the normal age of retirement and back to helping out part time, with the opportunity to indulge my pleasures - the lake, the boats and the walks, and present them all within this book. No longer the urge to strive for the highest peaks but now in the company of my wife and grandchildren and at a more leisurely pace with the time to stop and look around I have rediscovered paths from early childhood and many more besides.

The walks at an unhurried pace take from one hour up to 4½ hours and are not at all difficult. Along lake shores and the banks of rivers they follow fairly level ground and nowhere do they reach a height of more than 1000ft. The lake is the ideal place to enjoy the magnificent views of this beautiful area, within just a few minutes the walks take you in to peaceful surroundings where you will appreciate the scenery from a different aspect.

Jim Fleming

Whatever the season - snowdrops and daffodils of springtime - butterflies and scents of high summer - falling leaves and colours of autumn - clear days and crunchy snow in winter - leave the car behind and come and enjoy the lake and the real pleasures the area has to offer. We guarantee you will want to return again and again.

Finsthwaite - High Dam - Steam Railway

A walk from Lakeside through pleasant woodlands and meadows to Finsthwaite - High Dam and Newby Bridge and Steam Railway. (ask for timetable). Walking Time 2½ hours

1. Start this walk from Lakeside Steamer Pier. From the car park walk past Lakeside Hotel to main road and turn right. Walk 400 metres towards Hawkshead and you will find the public footpath on the left opposite the property signed "Buck Yeats North". It is a very rough track through coppiced woodland, ignore any forks left. Pass over a stone stile and head straight across two fields towards Finsthwaite Church clearly seen ahead. Follow the path onto a road to the left of the church and when

2

you are opposite the church take the first road left. This meets the village road in 50 metres. Turn right and your path is 20 metres on the left through the gates and driveway of the cottage "Plum Green". Walk straight through, noting yellow arrows directing you through a field to a small gate on the other side. As you come through the gate the path veers at a 45° angle right past a blue static caravan, look for white arrow painted on rock. It now heads straight for bridge over stream by the edge of deciduous woodland. Cross the bridge. You are now in a special conservation area managed by the National Park Authority.

2. The quick way is to walk left up the path to the tarns, do a circular tour and return the same way retracing your path to Lakeside, the total time taken would be no more than 1½ hours.

3. We recommend you turn right and descend 200 metres to entrance gates from car park. Go through and turn left into car park and you will see a kissing gate at the far end.

4. This path meanders amongst deciduous woodland, through a gap in a stone wall, through a kissing gate, sometimes rising and then descending until after 10 minutes it meets an old bridle path. Join the bridle path by rustic steps and turn left, it now climbs steadily between moss-covered walls until you reach two old and redundant gate stoops, where it becomes more open but still clearly defined. Another path coming up from the right joins by a wooden gate. Turn left and continue, steadily rising until you reach the access area to High Dam.

5. You enter the access area through a kissing gate and turn immediately right to follow the path around the tarn anti-clockwise. Don't worry if the path seems distant from the Tarn at first, it crosses open ground and then rises via a footbridge to reach a fine view point. To carry on you now descend and go over a small bridge (ignore the public footpath to Rusland), cross over a similar bridge and now meander along the edge of the tarn until you reach the walled dam itself, walk along the dam.

6. The actual circuit around the tarn, surprisingly, need only take twenty minutes. However we have not come across an area with so many peaceful resting places and you are well advised to allow time for this.

7. After walking across the dam descend by the path until you come to the wooden footbridge and cross the river again from where you entered this conservation area.

8. Retrace your steps through the field heading to the left of the isolated blue caravan, through gate and on into Finsthwaite and back to the

church. Carry straight on the way you came if you want the shortest route to Lakeside.

9. Alternative route to include a short ride on the steam railway if its running (ask for timetable on the day). Now look for footpath for Newby Bridge through iron kissing gate on the right into field. Walk straight up the middle of the longest part of the field towards a gap in the trees on the distant skyline. Cross by stile and keep going straight on following yellow arrows and crossing two more fields by stiles until you come to a wood at the end, now look for a stile at the right-hand corner of the field.

10. Cross into woodland and follow path left. It is very clear and soon descends to a drive which leads direct to the main Newby Bridge to Lakeside road. The Swan Hotel is 50 metres to the right. Check your watch! Check your train times! If you're going to stop for refreshments you will need to allow time to walk the 250 metres down the road opposite the hotel, following river on your left to Newby Bridge Halt, where you will board your steam train back to Lakeside.

Finsthwaite - Stott Park Bobbin Mill

The first part of this walk is described in walk 1, paragraph 1.

1. After entering the special conservation area, turn right and descend 200 metres to car park. Carry on down the driveway and join the main road. Turn left for 50 metres and look for off-road footpath on the right. Follow this path and it leads to the entrance to Stott Park Bobbin Mill. See Page 40.

2. After visiting the bobbin mill you will find the main road back to Lakeside further along where you turn right and it is approximately half a mile. It is a very busy road and you need to take great care if you choose to return this way.

3. You may retrace your steps via Finsthwaite, or pick up the walk to High Dam, in which case retrace your steps to the car park for High Dam. Look for the kissing gate at the far end and read now from Walk 1, paragraph 4.

High Dam - Photo: P. Southall

Stott Park Bobbin Mill - see Page 40

Lakeshore - Bowness to Lakeside

A walk on the quiet west shore using the Steamer/Launch to return. Three and a half hours walking via Finsthwaite, avoiding main roads.

From Mid-May to the end of September a traditional passenger launch service operates from Pier 3 at Bowness direct to Ferry House on the opposite shore and this is the preferred option to cross the lake. In the event of this service not being available directions to the car ferry are as follows.

From the piers at Bowness turn round and with your back towards the lake make for the corner on the right behind the Information Centre. Walk past Boatman's Cafe and along a road inaccessible to cars between the pitch and putt golf course and cemetery. Cross the road and take the footpath opposite, walking on past the public launch site at the Lake Wardens to the road and turn right down to Ferry Nab.

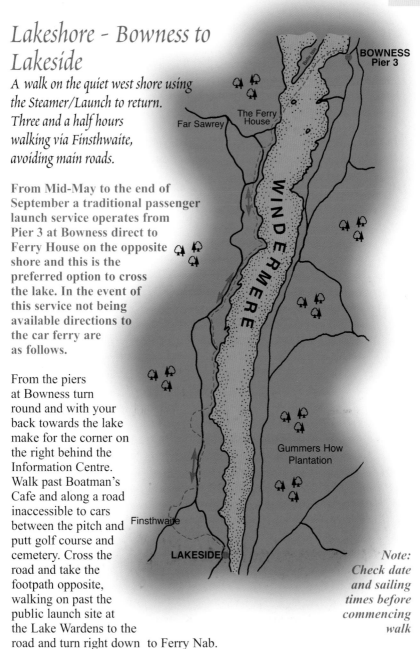

BOWNESS Pier 3

The Ferry House

Far Sawrey

WINDERMERE

Gummers How Plantation

Finsthwaite

LAKESIDE

Note: Check date and sailing times before commencing walk

6

1. When you reach the other side of the lake walk along the road until you come to the public footpath sign. This directs you away from the dangerously narrow roadway to Ash Landing. From Ash Landing car park cross the road and at the corner follow the track on the left by the lake shore for about 300 metres. The track then turns to the right avoiding private buildings and soon becomes a surfaced drive which in 200 metres meets a minor road. Turn left here. You will eventually pass a very large house by the lake - Fellborough - easily identified by the enormous conifers in the grounds. Just over 100 metres after the house cross a narrow stone stile and follow the path directly down to the lake shore and continue walking by the water's edge. Look ahead and you will see the curve of a peaceful tranquil bay terminating at a headland with a small island - Ling Holme 20 metres off shore. Make for the headland, the wooden footbridge crosses the River Cunsey, and you will find another bay which you follow round to Rawlinson Nab.

2. When you reach the other side of the Nab you walk by the edge of the lake with the water almost lapping at your feet. Unfortunately this is only for 200 metres and then the path turns away. Follow it up and over steps to a minor road.

3. Turn left and you will have to follow this road for approximately ⅓ of a mile (15 minutes) until you come to a public footpath sign on the left just over the brow of a long steep hill. This path now is through woodlands and gradually descends to the lake shore where you turn right. Look out for the yellow direction arrows as you go along but the path is quite distinct and keeps close to the water's edge.

4. The small island on the left is Silver Holme. Ducks, geese, swans and other water fowl frequent these quiet bays. Pheasant and other woodland birds and mammals are present all around.

5. The path abruptly meets a fence and you are now forced to move inland. Admire the view back up the lake before you leave it. You should be able to see Storrs Hall on the headland, part of Bowness to the left and above and beyond the beautiful Troutbeck Valley flanked by the pyramid shaped Ill Bell.

6. Turn left on the main road but only for 50 metres and join the footpath on the right, opposite the entrance to the YMCA. This path climbs into the woods but you should ignore any gates on the right and follow the fence until it comes down to the road again. Keep following the path by the road side until you are forced to join the road and then walk straight across and you will find the path continues just off the road on the other side.

7. You join the road again by Stott Park, Holidays in Lakeland, but 50 metres past this entrance look for a public footpath sign on the right. Walk up the driveway for 50 metres and then go left. You will see another sign directing you through a wooden gate into a field. The path crosses the field following the contour of the hill to a stone stile. Go straight on across the next field and into the corner to another stile which leads into woodland and on to finish at the road leading to the car park to High Dam.

8. Turn right on the main road to Finsthwaite and when you come to the first buildings take the lane left towards the church. Walk past the church and the school, now on your left, to the end of the lane and then straight on across two fields to join a stone stile into deciduous woodland. Follow the path straight on to join the main road. Turn right and walk along the road 400 metres until you come to Lakeside and the Lake Steamers if you wish to return to Bowness or Ambleside.

Lakeshore, Lakeside to Bowness   Walk 2A

An alternative start to walk no 2 from Lakeside. The first part of the walk is described in walk No 1, paragraph 1.

1. After entering the special conservation area, turn right and descend 200 metres to walk down the road past the car park. Just 20 metres before you reach the main road look out for a track on the left, it follows the wall at the end of the wood, with the field on the right. In less than 100 metres you will cross a stone stile into the corner of a field, follow the wall on the right for approximately 100 metres and then move towards the centre of the field and on to another stone stile. The path is not clear but keep going in the same direction and follow around the contour of the hill and then head for the right-hand corner where you will find a wooden gate.

2. The track leads 50 metres down to a drive, turn right and follow to the main road. On the main road turn left and walk past Stott Park - Holidays in Lakeland. Just past the entrance, on the right, there is an off-road footpath. This follows close to the road, it is quite muddy, and you will cross two pairs of wooden stiles until you are eventually forced back to the road again. Go straight across the road to the footpath on the other side.

3. You are now near the YMCA South Camp entrance and the footpath sign reads "880 yards". In just half this distance the footpath leads back to the road but ignore the road and go through the wooden kissing gate and follow the path upwards for 100 metres and then bear right following the fence on your left until you descend to the road again, opposite the entrance to YMCA National Centre.

4. If you turn left on the main road the public footpath to the lake shore is 50 metres past the YMCA entrance on the right hand side. When you reach the lake, a pleasant woodland path follows the lake shore for about 1 mile, detours, via a kissing gate, to avoid private land and then, after a short distance, turns abruptly left away from the shore. Follow the yellow arrows as the path climbs steadily through woodland for some ten to fifteen minutes and eventually meets a quiet country road. Turn right and follow the road down a long steep hill then walk on for a further half mile until you reach the signpost - Cunsey. Just past the first group of cottages - Holmewell House - turn right over a wooden stile and follow the path down to the lake shore.

5. Now follow the path by the water's edge for a further mile, via Rawlinson Nab with its sheltered picnic beaches, around the next bay to the island of Ling Holme 20 metres off shore. Cross the River Cunsey and continue to the far end of the next bay, then up to rejoin the quiet road. Turn right and walk past the large house - Fellborough - with its enormous conifers. 400 metres further on, at the bottom of a hill, turn right down the driveway - Bryers Cottage.

6. Walk down the Private Drive for 150 metres and follow the track alongside the lake which leads to the main road. If you cross the road to Ash Landing Car Park, there is a short off road path via "West's Station" and on to the ferry. If the traditional launch service is available you are advised to use it as it will take you directly to Bowness Bay.

7. If the launch service is not operating use the car ferry and after crossing over walk along the road and look for the path by the Lake Wardens and Public Slipway. A five minute walk leads directly to the steamer pier.

Lakeshore, Cunsey and Sawrey

A Walk on the quiet west shore from Bowness using the traditional launch service from Pier 3. Approximately three hours walking from Ferry House (extended by 20 minutes to include Hill Top).

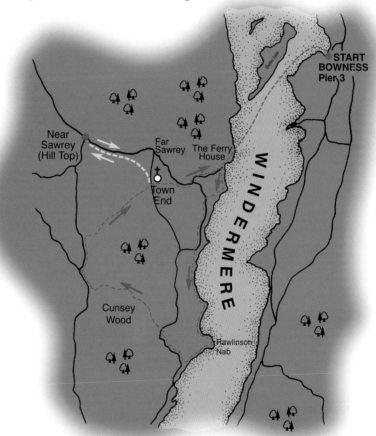

To commence this walk follow details of ferry crossing and paragraphs 1 - 2 of Walk 2 until you come to a minor road.

1. Turn right and walk for ½mile until you reach Cunsey Farm and then take the forest track opposite the farm entrance. After approximately five minutes walking mainly through a spruce plantation you will come down to the River Cunsey again. You do not cross now but follow the path to the left (yellow arrow) upstream and gradually it moves away from the

river. You will soon reach the open scrubland, don't go through the field but carry straight on. Walk for ¼mile, it can be quite muddy in places, and you will come to a minor road. Turn right and walk to the stone house which you can see. Immediately past the house turn right up the single track road and you will cross the River Cunsey. The river comes from Esthwaite Water, a small lake between Hawkshead and Near Sawrey.

2. You are now walking alongside a very long field and when you reach the end of the field you will see a public footpath on the right through woodland. Follow it in the direction of the yellow arrow and when you come to the end of the wood, cross the wooden stile and the path goes straight down through the fields. You cross another stile and go through a gate, keep straight on by the fence until you meet the road by a small white cottage. To extend the walk and visit Near Sawrey and Hill Top, read *"Extended Walk"*.

3. To return direct to Bowness, St Peter's Church, Town End, is straight ahead, turn left on the road for 20 metres and then ascend the hill by the path in front of the church and keep going until you come to the road, and turn right.

4. You are now at the top of the ferry hill and you will need to follow the main road down. Look out for the second junction on the right and there is a short distance with safe off-road footpath first on the right-hand side and then crossing over to the left-hand side and on to the ferry.

5. If the launch service is available you are advised to use it as it will take you directly to Bowness Bay

6. If the launch service is not operating use the car ferry and after crossing over walk along the road and look for the path by the Lake Wardens and Public Slipway. A five minute walk leads directly to the Steamer pier.

Extended Walk (Yellow route and arrows on map Page 10).
This walk may be extended to Near Sawrey if you walk past St Peter's Church for 60 metres and take the footpath left through a wooden kissing gate. This is a 10 minute walk through fields alongside a stream until it meets the road near Hill Top and the Tower Bank Arms. Retrace your steps to the church when you are ready to return.

Bowness Pier to Near Sawrey
(Hill Top - The House of Beatrix Potter)
and the Tarns

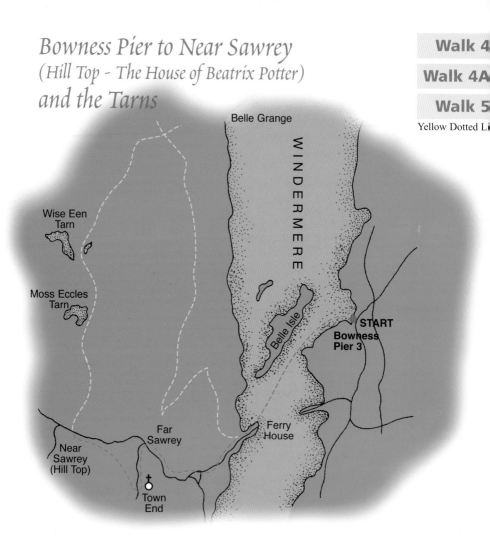

As with walks 2 and 3 you need to cross the lake in order to reach Hill Top and therefore we refer you to details of ferry crossings in the opening paragraph of Walk 2. The traditional launch takes only 10 minutes from Pier 3 at Bowness to the other side and you will find the boat combines with a bus service when you arrive at Ferry House. The bus from Ferry House takes a further 10 minutes to Hill Top before going on to Hawkshead and if you wish to travel this way we recommend you purchase a combined ticket. If you prefer to walk to Hill Top remember the road is narrow and dangerous in places and off road footpaths have been created for your safety and enjoyment so please use them where possible. Walking time approx. 45-50 minutes. **For details of Hill Top see Page 38.**

Ferry House to Hill Top - 45/50 minutes.

1. Disembarking from the passenger ferry or the car ferry walk past the public toilets - Bus stop is here - and follow the road around for 100 metres and look for the footpath on the right, yellow arrow and signed (Hill Top via Sawrey, Ash Landing, Claife Station). Walk on to a road and turn left - white arrow - walk around the corner and at the road juntion look for the footpath on the right with yellow arrow to Claife Station. Go on up towards the ruins of the station (see page 40) and turn left down the stepped path to Ash Landing to carry on walking through the car park. Follow the path upwards and straight on, after 200 metres it crosses the road and continues up on the other side until you reach the road again.

2. From the sign 'Far Sawrey' walk up the road for 150 metres to find the path again on the right. It is now straightforward and when you reach the highest level - 'Sawrey Knotts'- you should be able to see the top of Coniston Old Man straight ahead. Keep straight on and follow the lane down to meet the road by the Sawrey Hotel. Hill Top is signed '½mile in next village' but you can avoid the main road again if you turn down the road immediately opposite the Sawrey Hotel and follow this until just before the large church on the hill you will find a path on the right through the fields which will take you a further 10 minutes gentle stroll to Hill Top and the Tower Bank Arms which is handy for refreshments.

Hill Top to Ferry House - 45/50 minutes.

1. From the Bus Stop at Hill Top walk back past the house of Beatrix Potter and you will find the footpath 100 metres on the right signed to Ferry via Far Sawrey, after a short distance ignore the path on the left back to the road and walk on with the small stream on your left. When you reach the cottages with St Peter's Church straight ahead turn left on the road and carry on past the farm buildings and fork right up the hill to join the main road opposite Sawrey Hotel. Turn right and in 50 metres only the footpath forks left and you need to be 20 metres up the path in order to see the sign (do not follow the sign with blue arrow).

2. Walk Straight up past Sawrey Knotts and keep straight on and down until you meet the main road. Turn left and you will find the path 150 metres down on the right. Carry on and then cross the road, the path now on the left will lead through Ash Landing car park and upwards and on towards Claife Station. Turn right just before the ruins and down to meet the road. At the road fork left and the footpath is on the right in 50 yards to avoid the traffic.

Ferry Details - refer to paragraphs 5-6 at the end of walk 3 page 11.

Hill Top, The Tarns and Claife Heights

A 3¹/₄ Hours walk along Bridleways via Moss Eccles and Wise Een Tarns along forest paths to Claife Heights with views over the lake and finish at the Ferry.

1. From the bus stop at Near Sawrey walk along the road past Tower Bank Arms for 50 metres to turn right along the tarmac road and carry on past the farm buildings to join a bridleway. Turn left along the next bridleway, which joins from Far Sawrey. A 10-minute walk along this gradually ascending track will bring you to the first of the tarns, Moss Eccles, with its reed covered banks sheltering many species of water fowl.

Wise Een Tarn - Photo: M. A. Fleming

2. A further 10 minutes of similar terrain will bring you to Wise Een Tarn with the beautiful view across to the Langdale Pikes. Carry on between the tarns, the smaller tarn on the right is unnamed as far as we know, and ascend to a conifer plantation. Once into the plantation the path levels for a short distance before descending. Ignore the path on the left and descend 200 metres to a way marker with a white-topped post and turn right signed 'Ferry and Far Sawrey.'

3. The path goes through the trees and is clearly marked all the way by white posts. The ground is forever covered with tree roots, rocks and muddy areas so boots are essential. You will soon emerge into a new plantation by Post No. 7. Turn right and carry on to the top of the hill, walking forward to the large rock to admire the view.

Look left to see where the lake begins at Waterhead with Ambleside village beyond nestling in the valley below the Fairfield Horseshoe. As your eye moves right Wansfell and the Troutbeck valley stand out and then on to the villages of Windermere and Bowness so quiet and peaceful from here.

4. Now continue down along the path until you join the forestry road at Post No. 6 turn right for less than 100 metres and go left at Post No. 5. There are various paths off to view points along the way, take them by all means but make sure you retrace your steps to the main white post trail. You will meet the path coming from Belle Grange at Post No. 4 turn right.

5. Soon the rough muddy path gives way to easier conditions and after going through a gate into open land becomes a rough track again, after some distance this leads down to Post No. 3. Turn left and you are no longer following signs for Hill Top, Sawrey but now the Ferry. In less than 5 minutes turn right at Post No. 2.

6. You will come to the point of descent in approx. 10 minutes. The path zig zags steeply down to West's Station (see page 40) walk through the ruins and turn left down to the road. At the road fork left and the footpath is on the right in 50 yards to avoid the traffic.

7. If the launch service is available you are advised to use it as it will take you directly to Bowness Bay.

8. If the launch service is not operating use the car ferry and after crossing over walk along the road and look for the path by the Lake Wardens and Public Slipway. A five minute walk leads directly to the Steamer pier.

Wray Castle to the Ferry

A gentle stroll of no more than 1¹/₂ hours along paths and tracks by the quiet western shore of Windermere, or detour for Claife ridge and the walk becomes 2¹/₂ hours with magnificent views and varied, easy to follow, forest paths.

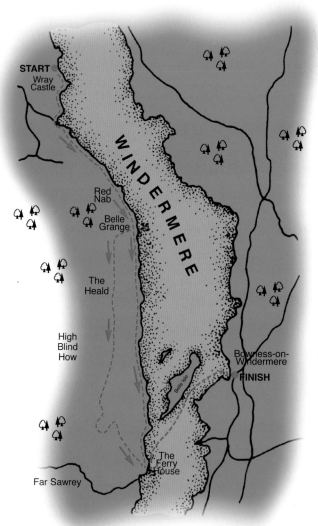

Introduction

Every day from Easter until the end of October, a launch service departs hourly from Waterhead to Brockhole starting at 9.45am, with the last boat at 4.45pm. This will drop you, by request, at Wray Castle, all you have to do now is walk either the low level or high level path to Ferry House and the crossing to Bowness where a Steamer or Sightseeing Cruiser will return you to Waterhead. If you start the day from Lakeside or Bowness change boats at Waterhead but don't forget, - ask to get off at Wray Castle. The three boat trips are all included with the discounted 'Walkers Ticket'.

When you step off the little jetty at Wray, you need to take the path left to follow the lake shore. However if you wish to visit the castle first, it is only a few minutes detour along the path leading away from the lake. Details of the castle can be found on page 40. Retrace your steps to commence the walk.

1. Follow the lakeside path past the black painted wooden boathouse. The woods are full of birdlife and it is difficult to imagine you are beside the busiest lake as you wander in such a peaceful environment. The path is well defined and, when you reach the end of the wood, cross the stile to a field and follow it down to the water's edge. As you make your way around the bay you will see two small stone boathouses. After passing the first, move towards the gate on the right, to avoid swampy ground, and turn left onto a well defined track passing through Claife Estate. After approximately 20 minutes the track meets a road, but don't worry - it is unsurfaced as it is the policy of the National Trust, who own this land, to discourage motorists and keep it peaceful and quiet. After passing the white house "Belle Grange", you may continue along this track beside the lake for about an hour until you reach the ferry and don't forget to catch the traditional launch service to Bowness as its included in your ticket and the car ferry isn't.

2. If you would like to walk the Claife Ridge, take the roughly paved bridleway signposted "Latterbarrow, Hawkshead and Near Sawrey". Five hundred years ago this bridleway was linked by ferry to Millerground across the lake and was the trading route from Hawkshead to Kendal (Windermere as a village did not exist). Climb steadily through mature deciduous woodland for approximately ten minutes and, where the path forks, go left following "Public Footpath - Far Sawrey". You are now faced with a further twenty minutes unrelenting climb until the path levels and meets more open ground. Now you can enjoy the views across the lake, Troutbeck on the left, Windermere village and beyond Belle Isle, Bowness and the boat landings.

3. These woods are home to many species of wild birds, some rarely seen in populated areas are numerous in the quietness of the mixed woodlands on this side of Windermere. Deer, both red and fallow, roam freely over large areas of these woodlands, look for evidence of their passing, you will be lucky to see the animals themselves.

4. The path continues on this high level for approximately ten minutes and then turns away from the lake into a dense spruce plantation, and then left as it meets another path and this is POST 4 on the white trail. Carry straight on and then read on from Paragraph 5 from Walk No 5.

Roman Fort and River Banks to Ambleside or Rydal

A walk following lake shore, visiting Roman Fort "Galava" and by river banks to Ambleside, approximately 1 hour circular route, or an extended walk including Rydal of 2½ hours circular route.

1. Leave the pier at Waterhead and turn left to walk to the end of the promenade. Join the pavement and walk 100 metres passing the Wateredge Inn and enter Borrans Park, following the path down to the shore of the lake. The park is maintained by South Lakeland District

Council and, although it is only for a short distance, it is delightful to walk by the small sandy beaches, reed beds and picnic sites. Walk around but before the path leaves the park, cut across the grass to the gate and enter Galava, Ambleside Roman Fort - see page 37.

River Rothay - P. Southall

2. Galava site is in the custody of the National Trust. There is an explanatory plaque by the gate and at each of the excavations and it only takes a few moments to browse around. You should head to the left of the fenced off excavations. NOTE the plaque Porta Principalis and carry on from here towards the river and pass through a gate to the boardwalk and path; follow the river upstream until you come to the road. Ignore the footbridge left as you go through the gate but join the main road and cross carefully to the other side. Going left walk around the Rothay Manor Hotel, following signs "Town Centre - Keswick (A591)", immediately past Riverside Lodge Hotel turn left into entrance signed "Lorry, Coach & Car Park". You will find the public footpath sign beside the river 50 metres behind the Ambulance Station. Follow the river upstream until you come to Rothay Park, cross the stile and stay by the river until you reach Miller Bridge.

3. **For Ambleside Village.** Turn right through the park, pass to the left of St. Mary's Church and a further 50 metres brings you into Compston Road. The one way traffic system will take you through the village centre and directly back to Waterhead for the boats in approximately 15 minutes.

   For Rydal. Leave the park, walking across Miller Bridge to join the road and turn right, cross over a cattle grid and continue along this road for approximately one mile. You are still close to the river, now on your right, and the road is closed to cars unless they are using it for access. It should be mainly traffic free but you will need to take care and be aware of the occasional vehicle. This quiet road comes to an end as you cross another cattle grid approaching Pelter Bridge.

4. **For Rydal.** Go across the bridge and join the main road (A591). Turn left and follow pavement 200 metres before crossing the very busy road to Rydal Mount.

5. You will find your return footpath near the entrance to Rydal Hall, walk along the track behind the Hall and if you are looking for one of those idyllic locations for a break visit the teashop here by the river. Rydal Hall is owned by the Diocese of Carlisle see page 39.

6. The footpath is now well signed and follows a rough drive, fenced both sides, through Rydal Park for approximately one mile. The drive abruptly comes to an end as it meets the A591 and you need to cross to the pavement and turn left for Ambleside. Walk for 400 metres and you will reach the village. The Armitt Ambleside Museum is here on the left. To avoid the village centre look for the footpath to Miller Bridge, it's opposite the Health Centre, turn right down Stoney Lane and when you come to Miller Bridge do not cross but follow the path through Rothay Park you are now retracing your steps following the river downstream continue until you come to the road. Turn right down the access road and right again on to the main road, walking against the one-way traffic system, pass Riverside Lodge Hotel on the right and Rothay Manor on the left. Do not cross the bridge on the right but walk round Rothay Manor and after 50 metres turn right onto a public footpath. Again do not cross the bridge but enter the field by the gate alongside and walk to the riverbank. Follow the river until you come back to the remains of the Roman fort and then on into Borrans Park. If you follow the path towards the lake you will soon be able to see across to the piers at Waterhead and watch for your boat coming in to take you back to Bowness or Lakeside.

Borrans Park - P. Southall

Grasmere - Dove Cottage

A walk visiting the Roman Fort "Galava" and by riverbank and lakeshore paths to Grasmere & Dove Cottage, one way 3 hours - return 5 hours.

The walk starts at Waterhead Pier and the directions to Pelter Bridge are as for Walk 7, Paragraphs 1 to 3, missing out the directions for Ambleside.

1. After crossing the cattle grid turn left **for Grasmere** before Pelter Bridge and walk up the road over another cattle grid keeping the river on your right. Walk past the car park, the road rises and winds upwards until you reach a pair of stone cottages. Take the path on the right through the wood and down to join the river. Follow this upstream and in 50 metres you will see Rydal Water. The path leads through Rydal Woods and soon reaches and follows the lake shore. After approximately half an hour you will be faced with a short but steep rise and rewarded with a fine view over Grasmere. Take the path down towards the river and go left along the lake shore and continue with the lake on your right for some twenty minutes. The path leaves the lake, turning abruptly left by a small footbridge to join the road by way of a wooden stile. Turn right and follow the road into Grasmere village.

2. From Grasmere there are two options.

    A. Look for the bus stop and the open topped service by Stagecoach will take you to Waterhead for your return boat journey.

    B. Walk on the B5287 past the church and car park on your left and cross the main A591 to reach Dove Cottage - See Page 37.

    Walk along Stock Lane rising all the time, at the clearing ignore the road to Rydal and carry on up the hill marked "Path to Rydal". Shortly after the top of the hill the road levels and you will see Rydal Water on your right. Carry straight on and the tarmac road gives way to a track which, after approximately half an hour, leads to Rydal Mount. See Page 39.

3. Your footpath to Ambleside is a short way down on the left by the entrance to Rydal Hall. Read now from Paragraph 5, Walk 7.

Ambleside and Waterfalls

A circular walk of 2 to 2¹/₂ hours through woodlands, the byways of Old Ambleside, waterfalls, riverbanks and lake shore.

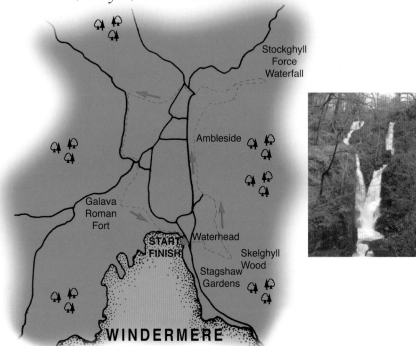

1. From the piers at Waterhead cross the main A591 road by the corner of the Waterhead Hotel and take the public footpath marked to Jenkins Crag. The path is rough and quite steep at first, then it levels out and crosses a field into woodland. Follow it up into the woods for just over 100 metres and look carefully for the turning left, it is not too obvious at first, but after a short distance the path soon becomes clear and as it leaves Skelghyll Woods it joins a rough track. Go left and admire the view across the lake head and the ancient Roman Fort of Galava. The track soon meets a surfaced roadway, carry straight on down towards the village and you will see the garden centre below.

2. The first road you come to is the Old Lake Road and you turn right onto it (the main road runs parallel to it but we wish to avoid that). Follow the road past the car park on your left, past Fisherbeck Lane and then Blue Hill Road on your right, then take the next right turn up Low Gale Road

22

(marked "No Through Road"). After 150 metres, ignore the path down to the village and follow the sign for Stockghyll and Wansfell which points up the road "Gale Howe Park'. In another 50 metres you will see the footpath going left. Follow this path until you come out onto a driveway "Havenwood" and carry on left between high beech hedges until you come to the road then turn left. You should by now be aware of the sound of rushing water and as you walk down the road you will catch your first sight of the waterfalls to the right. The entrance to Stock Ghyll Park is only 200 metres away (see Page 40).

3. The walk through the woods is a delight at any time of year. Birds, flowers, squirrels, tumbling waters all within a few hundred yards of one of Lakeland's busiest villages. Whenever the path forks keep to the higher levels on the right and walk to the top of the falls. A wooden foot-bridge crosses the river here and the path brings you back down the other side. The full circuit need only take thirty minutes but this is not a walk to hurry and there are many view points and resting places.

4. When you are ready to leave, join the road again and continue down until you come to the main road in the village. You may go left through the village centre, and the main road will bring you back to Waterhead and the piers. However if you want to avoid the village turn right on the main road, walk past the market cross and the shopping precinct, (the Bridge House is approximately 100 metres further along the main road), and turn down Compston Road for 50 metres and follow sign right for Rothay Park and Loughrigg. Walk on past St. Mary's Church and through the park until you come to the river.

5. Do not cross the bridge but follow the path left alongside the riverbank. When you reach the end of the park cross over a wooden stile and continue until you come to the road. Turn right down the access road and right again onto the main road, walking against the one way traffic system pass Riverside Lodge Country Hotel on the right and Rothay Manor Hotel on the left. Do not cross the bridge on the right but walk round Rothay Manor and after 50 metres turn right onto a public footpath. Again do not cross the bridge but enter the field by the gate alongside and walk to the riverbank. Follow the river downstream through two fields and carry on alongside the riverbank eventually coming to a wooden boardwalk over the worst of the muddy ground. Enter the field and walk past the remains of Galava, the Roman Fort, to an iron kissing gate to enter Borrans Park. Follow the path towards the lake and you will soon be able to see across to the piers at Waterhead and watch for your boat coming in to take you back to Bowness or Lakeside.

Waterhead Pier to Orrest Head, Windermere and Bowness

A 4¹/₂ hour walk through Woodlands and the Troutbeck Valley with spectacular Lake and Mountain views and a lakeshore path.

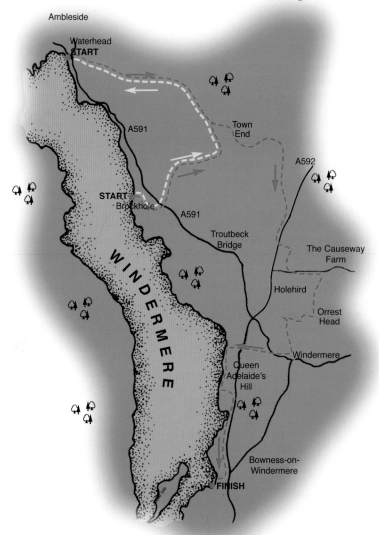

1. From the piers at Waterhead cross the main A591 road by the corner of the Waterhead Hotel and take the public footpath marked to Jenkins Crag. The path is rough and quite steep at first, then it levels out and crosses a field into woodland. Follow it up into the woods bearing right. A National Trust sign "Kelsick Scar" is reached after 20 minutes. The ground levels out at this point and, 60 metres ahead, is Jenkins Crag, a magnificent Windermere viewpoint. Retrace your steps to the path and carry on along the track marked "Troutbeck via Robin's Lane".

2. Twenty minutes further on is High Skelghyll Farm. Go through the farm and after 100 metres cross a cattle grid. The path swings away to the left, follow it upwards for fifteen minutes to reach Robin's Lane. Carry on along this lane for 2-3 minutes and you will meet another lane on the right leading up from Brockhole.

3. Walk 11 joins here but you go straight on for about 300 metres until you come to a wooden seat at the viewpoint.A bridleway leads down to the right and if you follow this you will reach a road in five minutes. Turn left and pick up the bridleway again on the right after 100 metres. Follow this down to a white cottage, Town Foot, (to visit Town End see Page 40, detour left 100 metres and retrace your steps), cross the road and follow down to the river.

4. Here the river Troutbeck is crossed by two wooden footbridges (during late autumn large salmon and sea trout can be seen as they make their long journey from the sea, through the lake and up to their spawning grounds high in the Troutbeck valley). Go through the gate and follow the path up to the top of the field. the road is the A592 from Windermere to Ullswater. Turn right and follow the footpath along by the roadside for 400 metres, then cross the road to a kissing gate and public footpath which leads upwards through two fields. Look out for Annies Seat and enjoy the splendid view across the lake to Coniston and Wetherlam.

5. Go over a wooden stile and continue between buildings to the road, cross into the lane and go on over a cattle grid and after 100 metres fork left. You are now on a surfaced farm road which you follow for 400 metres. When you reach the farm, walk past the first building and look for a wooden stile on the right. Cross and go through the farm yard looking out for yellow direction arrows. Cross the next two fields looking out for stiles and yellow direction arrows until you arrive at white farm cottages. Proceed down the lane to the road and turn left. This is Crosses Farm. Follow this road and in 400 metres you will come to Causeway Farm. Ignoring the footpath opposite continue for a further 200 metres where there is a better and more direct path on the other side of a small tarn. The path is marked 'public footpath' and you cross the wall on the

right by a stone stile. Keep close to wall on the right and in 50 metres cross the small stream and continue for a further 50 metres only before heading for the highest point ahead. The path is not obvious for some distance but if you keep about 100 metres to the left of the wall you will find it soon becomes clearer the more you progress and by the time you come to cross a stone stile, where the walls join, it is indeed now very clear to the summit. This is Orrest Head, and the view is breathtaking over the full length of the lake and away beyond to the Lakeland Fells. This is the view that inspired Wainwright on his first visit to the Lake District.

6. From the summit take any path down as they all lead to Windermere village. Coming off Orrest Head you join the main road opposite the Railway Station and Booth's Supermarket. To avoid the village turn right and follow the main road towards Ambleside, keeping to the pavement. In 300 metres you will come to St. Mary's Church and just past the Church the footpath down to Millerground. Follow this path down until you come to a main road. Cross with great care and opposite is the path to Queen Adelaide's Hill. Twenty metres to the right is the path to Millerground. This path leads down to the lake shore.

7. Follow the path along the lake shore, past the piers and the picnic site, almost as far as it is possible to go and near the end look out for inscription on a rock at the right hand side - re Queen Adelaide's Hill page 39. Go through the iron gate at the end and cross the field to the road and the pavement on the far side. Turn right and walk for 15 to 20 minutes passing the steamboat museum until you reach Bowness village and the promenade for cruises to Ambleside or Lakeside.

Brockhole to Orrest Head, Windermere and Bowness

A 4 to 4½ hour walk through woodlands and the Troutbeck Valley with spectacular lake and mountain views and a lake-shore path.

1. Take a Windermere Lake Cruises launch from Bowness or Waterhead to Brockhole Jetty and walk up through the grounds and car park to the main A591 road. Cross the road to the bus stop on the right hand side and follow the waymark sign (blue arrow) up Mirk Lane. The track leads up through woodlands and, after about ten minutes, reaches Wood Farm where it diverts right, around a stone wall. Turn left along a tarmac road for 50 metres, then continue on a path following the blue arrows. There is at first a steep ascent for two to three minutes until the track makes a hairpin turn left. Turn right on the bend towards a wooden gate leading into a country lane, there is a gradual climb after this for about ten minutes until you join a minor road at Castle Syke Farm, where you bear to the right for thirty metres before joining a footpath again going left and upwards.

2. There now follows a steady climb for approximately ten minutes where you will pass over two wooden stiles, it can be quite muddy here. At the second stile you should see a National Trust sign "Martins Wood", a further five minutes brings you to a wooden gate with stile alongside leading into a lane where you turn right and "Robin's Lane" is twenty metres further on. Turn right when you reach 'Robin's Lane' and continue the walk referring to Paragraph 3 of previous Walk 10.

Note: The viewpoint (see Page 29) is approximately 200 metres left along Robin's Lane towards Waterhead. If the weather conditions are clear you may wish to divert and then retrace your steps.

Brockhole to Waterhead

A two hour walk through woodlands and bridleways with spectacular Lake and Mountain views.

To start this walk refer to paragraphs 1 & 2 of walk no 11.

1. Turn left when you reach Robin's Lane and within 100 metres you should see the view of Wansfell straight ahead. At the kissing gate there is a signpost "Skelghyll via Jenkins Crag". Turn left again, following the blue arrow. You will now begin to appreciate the efforts you have made to gain this high ground as you look out over the head of the lake to breathtaking views of Coniston Old Man, Bowfell, Scafell and the Langdale Pikes. (Why not take time off for ten minutes to rest and take photographs?). From Brockhole to this point you will normally take one hour.

2. Continue to descend the path crossing two small streams until you reach the hollow. Here there are two wooden gates and a footbridge, cross the river and turn right over the cattle grid and follow a tarmac track, now marked by a yellow arrow, up and through a farm to join a bridleway. After a few minutes you begin a descent through deciduous woodland - Kelsick Scar. This soon leads to Jenkins Crag where a short detour, for the magnificent view across Windermere and lengthways down the lake to Bowness and beyond, is strongly recommended.

3. Rejoin the path which meanders on to the village of Ambleside, or, for a more direct route to the lake, head straight down to the bottom of the woods, cross over the wooden stile and the field straight ahead, cross another stile and follow the clearly defined path down to the main road. You will see Waterhead Pier opposite with the welcoming Steampacket Restaurant where you may refresh yourself prior to catching a steamer or launch to return to Bowness or Lakeside.

Panoramic view of the Langdale Pikes and Lakeland Fells from near 'Robins' Lane' - Walks 10 - 12. This view is also enjoyed from the decks of Steamers or Launches en route Bowness to Ambleside.

The Viewpoints Over Windermere

A short walk of one hour around Post Knott and Biskey Howe, or an extended walk of three to four hours including Post Knott, School Knott and Biskey Howe.

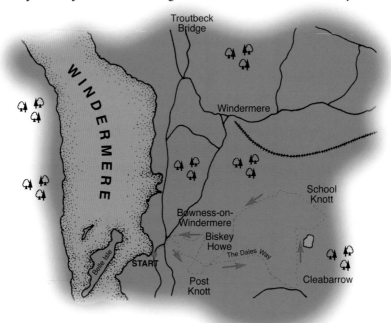

1. From the piers at Bowness make your way into the village and go past the roundabout to the top of the hill (Crag Brow). Opposite the entrance to the Beatrix Potter Centre look for Langrigg Drive. Walk along Langrigg Drive (it's only about 400 metres) and when you reach the end turn left up a steep hill. This road comes to an end in about 150 metres where you pass through a small iron gate and proceed up past the "Dalesway" sign to join a well defined path where you turn right. (Towards the end of the walk you will return to this point and take the path in the opposite direction.) The path right is marked "Footpath Post Knott" and you follow this until you reach a wooden gate. Go through and ascend 100 metres to the viewpoint immediately in front. This is Post Knott, and from here you will see the lake spread below. Looking directly down to Bowness, pick out the Round House on Belle Isle and directly above and beyond Claife Heights you should also be able to see the mountain known as Coniston Old Man. Away to the left is the best view of the southern reaches of Windermere to Lakeside at the far end.

2. When you are ready to carry on turn around and, with your back to the lake, you will see a stone wall with a copse on the other side. Make your way to the left hand corner of this wall and cross the first stile. Ignoring the second stile, turn right and walk up between the wall and the copse to the top, crossing the wall to the left by another stone stile. The path marked by a yellow arrow leads down to a lane at the bottom. You are now some 30-45 minutes into the walk and the short version turns left at this point, in which event miss out paragraphs 3-6

3. For the main walk pass through the gate on the right, cross the farm drive, and go through the wooden gate into the field. Keep close to the wall on the right until you reach an iron gate. Go through and take the left fork in the path, continuing in the same general direction as before. You are on the Dalesway path and yellow arrows point the way. You will come to a road but as you approach you should see the path to the left on the other side. When you come to a farm lane you will need to cross by wooden gates and proceed upward through the field alongside the fence on the right. Cross the road and carry on over a small beck, straight on over a rise and along the lane until you reach the main road. You are going to turn left, but **do not** walk on the road as it is very dangerous. Just by the entrance you will find a stone stile and 300 metres of newly constructed safe pathway alongside the road. When you reach the end of this section to rejoin the road, you are immediately onto a surfaced lane going left. The Dalesway sign is now marked with a red arrow. Walk on past High Cleabarrow and after 200 metres the surfaced lane becomes a track. Go through the gate and a further three wooden gates, you will probably find it quite muddy. After crossing a small stream walk a further 200 metres and you will see the Dalesway sign (now yellow again) going right. The path is clearly marked and, although upwards, it is not steep and it is only half a mile to School Knott Tarn; a small stream is crossed on the way.

4. This is an ideal picnic spot, usually sheltered and peaceful and if time permits why not rest up? You should be two and a half hours into the walk with a further one and a half to go.

5. The path continues to the left of the tarn and half way along takes a sharp turn to the left. Go through the gate in the wall and straight on to the highest point. This is School Knott and from here look down on Windermere Village. The mountains dominate the view but it is the northern half of the lake, up to Waterhead, which takes the eye. To the right of the village you should be just able to see the traffic on the A591, Windermere - Kendal road and just beyond the mountains over the Troutbeck Valley, High Street and further right Kentmere.

6. The way is not clear from here, but head down towards the nearest group of houses. Just beyond a wooden gate the path forks. Take the left hand fork continuing towards the houses, just visible through the trees. When you come to the track turn left through another wooden gate past "Old Droomer" cottage on the left. Thirty metres further on turn right down some stone steps, cross the river and carry straight on for Lickbarrow. After crossing fields make for the corner of the wall and straight on over to join the road. The path continues straight across the road and through an iron gate, clearly marked "Public Footpath". Carry on past some houses, through a wooden gate, descend to reach the "Public Footpath Bowness" and turn left. You will come to 2 stiles, ignore the one straight ahead and take the one on the left again marked "public footpath". After about 300 metres go through a wooden gate with a farm just ahead. Pass the farm and follow the yellow arrows through two further gates. Look for the yellow arrow on the wall corner 50 metres ahead, and follow this across to another gate. Turn left onto the road and follow the markers through two more gates until you come to a track. Carry on through the gate and cross the farm lane again. You are now back at the junction where you joined earlier at paragraph 2.

7. Carry on for about 100 metres and you reach the path that leads up from the village, but this time turn right to follow the footpath marked "Bowness". In a short distance you come to the end of the path from Post Knott. Here turn left along the driveway and at the road junction go straight ahead for the viewpoint. After 100 metres follow the wheelchair accessible path which will take you to Biskey Howe. As you approach the large rock, bear right and you will find some stone steps under a large beech tree. Climb the steps, taking care as the rock can be very slippery. The view across Windermere is now dominated by the Langdale Pikes and just in front of the rock you will find a stone pedestal carrying a relief map to help you identify the various peaks.

8. Bowness village is just below you, with the whole 10½ miles of the lake spread out from Lakeside to Waterhead. We recommend that you savour the view, but after resting and refreshing yourselves can we suggest a cruise. as the perfect way to relax is to board one of our steamers or launches, enjoy a drink on board, and effortlessly take in those wonderful views from a different perspective.

9. To drag yourself away from this beautiful vantage point simply walk forward toward the seats and you will find a path on the left which meanders down through the rhododendrons and trees to join the road leading back to Crag Brow and the main road left back to the piers.

Fell Foot - Gummers How

Direct route and return 1¹/₂ hours, using forest paths via
Chapel House Plantation and return 3 hours.

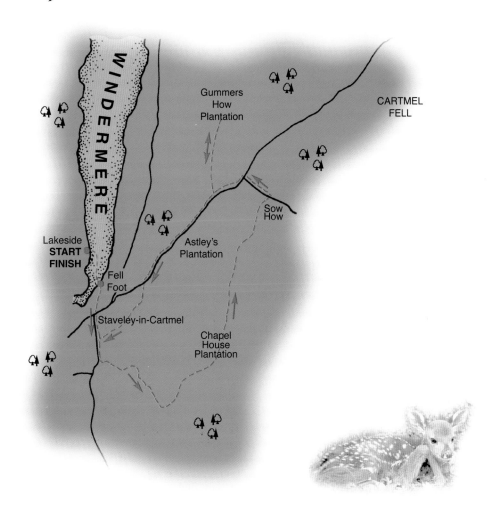

1. From Lakeside take the short ferry ride to Fell Foot and from the jetty make your way right to the car park exit. For the direct route turn left on the main road and walk for 100 metres to a road junction signed Gummers How. Three quarters of a mile steady climb up the hill will bring you to the well marked footpath to the summit. - see paragraph 4.

2. For the forest walk turn right at the car park exit and, after 50 metres, take the road to Staveley. Walk for a quarter of a mile until you come to a telephone kiosk and turn left along a public bridleway - Simpson Ground. After just over 200 metres you will come to a gate into a very muddy field. Enter and follow the path left, it is not very clear at first but meanders and then heads towards the top right hand side of the field where you will soon see a wooden gate. Go through and continue upwards following the blue arrows until you come to a forest road.

3. Turn left, now following the yellow arrows. When the road swings right carry straight on along a track into a spruce plantation. Soon the path forks, now ignoring the yellow arrows, take the left fork. The path is very muddy in places as it takes you into the heart of the forest for approximately half an hour until you reach another forest road. Turn left and you soon arrive at Sow How Lane. Turn left, then left again onto the main road. Two hundred metres over the brow of the hill you come to the footpath to Gummers How Summit.

4. The walk from here to Gummers How and back will take approximately 45 minutes allowing 10 minutes for views from the top - see page 37.

5. After descending to the road, cross to a footpath down to a car park, then follow the road down for just over half a mile. Take the public footpath to Staveley on the left, cross a stile and go straight on into the woods towards a wall on the left for approximately 100 metres, then follow the path down through newly planted trees until you come to a wall at the bottom. Cross a stone stile, following the path left, then on until you leave the spruce plantation. Cross another stile and go right, through a gate 20 metres ahead, and back into Staveley. Turn right for Fell Foot.

nurture lakeland

Nurture Lakeland was established in 1993 to bring together conservation organisations and businesses engaged in tourism. Our aim is to promote sustainable tourism by raising much needed funds for vital conservation projects in the Lake District. Businesses recognise the importance of contributing to the surrounding landscape and many operate visitor payback schemes/voluntary levies which benefit footpath repair, bridge restoration, habitat protection, woodland management and other similar projects.

Windermere England's largest lake, 10½ miles long, one mile wide at its widest point. The bed is owned by South Lakeland District Council, formerly by Windermere Urban District Council, and was acquired through the generosity of Henry Leigh Groves of Holehird on 5th April 1939.

The Lake District National Park was established in 1951, the first of the family of 11 National Parks in England and Wales, which in all cover about 10% of the country. The Lake District is the largest of these areas measuring 2292 sq. Km.

The Lake District National Park Authority is a local government body, funded by the taxpayer through central government, which aims to conserve and enhance the natural beauty, wildlife and cultural heritage of the Lake District; promote opportunities for the understanding and enjoyment of the special qualities of the National Park, and a duty to foster the economic and social well being of local communities within the National Park. It owns only 4% of the land in the park, and operates eight Tourist Information Centres, plus two in partnership and the Visitor Centre at Brockhole. It acts as the planning authority, making decisions on development and control applications and works very closely with other landowners including The National Trust, Forest Enterprise, and North West Water PLC in the repair and improvement of footpaths and drystone walls, the protection of flower meadows, woodlands and lakeshore habitats, the planting of trees and restoration of hedgerows. For further details telephone 01539 724555.

The National Trust was founded in 1895 to preserve places of historical interest or natural beauty permanently for the nation to enjoy. It is a registered charity, independent of government and relies on membership subscriptions, gifts, legacies and the contributions of many thousands of volunteers. Since the purchase of Brandlehow Park, on the shore of Derwentwater, in 1902, the trust has gradually, in just over 100 years, acquired ownership, or responsibility for the conservation and management of approximately one quarter of The Lake District National Park, and this in turn constitutes almost one quarter of the Trust's entire holding across England, Wales and Northern Ireland. For further details telephone 015394 35599.

English Heritage is a government funded organisation, established in 1986 to preserve and protect and make available to the public England's historic buildings and monuments.

Forest Enterprise
Forest Enterprise is responsible for the management of the Forestry Commissions forests throughout Great Britain. It provides many facilities for visitors including walking and cycling trails, sculptures, picnic sites and

guided walks. Forest Enterprise manages many sites in Cumbria, including Grizedale and Whinlatter Forest Parks. For further details please telephone 01229 860373.

The Armitt Ambleside Museum is where local history comes to life. Visitors are invited to take an interactive "birds eye" view of the Lakeland landscape through the magic of photographer Herbet Bell. A lantern slide show, an exhibition of Roman artefacts, Beatrix Potter's original natural history water colours and a variety of local history displays, are other attractions at this world famous heritage centre.

Biskey Howe, refer footpath walk 13. Early accounts of Windermere describe the "rugged crags of Biscot How", a high point above Bowness on Windermere, now better known as Biskey Howe. From the top there are excellent views across Bowness Bay and to Ambleside in the north.

Bridge House is sited on a bridge over Stock Ghyll in the centre of Ambleside and is used as a National Trust Information Centre. This tiny house was built in the 17th century, part of the Braithwaite Estate. It is believed to have been used as a summer house in the gardens of Ambleside Hall, prior to the building of the Ambleside to Grasmere turnpike road in 1834, which passed through the grounds surrounding the house. It was purchased through public subscription by the National Trust in 1926, at a cost of £450.

Brockhole was built in 1899 as a private home for the Gaddum family. The house was designed by Dan Gibson and the beautiful gardens laid out by Thomas Mawson, a renowned local landscape gardener. After the last war it became a convalescent home for Merseyside ladies, and was subsequently purchased by The Lake District National Park Authority in 1966. It opened as the country's first National Park Centre in 1969. The visitor Centre has exhibitions, regular audio visual shows and a changing programme of events, also an exciting adventure playground. Open daily, Easter to October inclusive, admission is free and there is a boat service from Bowness or Waterhead, May - October.

Claife Heights rise steeply from the western shore of Windermere, covered with forest plantations. The National Trust owns the land and have laid out a variety of walking trails through the woods and a lakeshore path from the ferry to Wray Castle. In 1794 John Curwen of Belle Isle obtained the land by private Act of Parliament. In 1798 30,000 larches were planted and in 1799 a quantity of oaks, while at the same time the flatter area at the top was converted into pasture and stocked with Shorthorn cattle. It was acquired by HM Treasury in lieu of death duties and given to the National Trust in 1962.

Dora's Field, sometimes known as Rashfield or Rushfield, is next to Rydal Mount. It was purchased by Wordsworth in 1826 for his daughter, Dora, and given to the National Trust by his grandson, Gordon Wordsworth, in 1935. The Trust grant free access at all times of the year. The steeply sloping field with its network of walkways is famous for its daffodils in Spring and views across Rydal Water. Access is via a gate at the northern corner of St. Mary's Church, Rydal.

Dove Cottage was William Wordsworth's home between 1799 and 1808. He lived there with his sister Dorothy, and during that period wrote many of his best poems and the fourteen books of "The Prelude". The house and museum are open to the public. The museum houses a permanent exhibition on the life and works of the poet and holds a programme of special exhibitions throughout the year. The pretty cottage garden at the rear was tended by Wordsworth himself and has been partially restored.

Fellfoot Park and Gardens were formerly the private estate of Colonel Ridehalgh, the first man to own a private steamer on the lake (Fairy Queen, 1860). Although the main house was demolished many years ago, the boathouse and dock have been preserved. The property has been owned by the National Trust since 1948 and was opened to the public in 1973 as a leisure centre. A regular ferry service from Lakeside connects with the lake steamers.

Galava Roman Fort was one of a line of Roman forts linking Kendal (Watercrook) with Ravenglass via Hardknott Pass. The first wooden fort was constructed at the head of Windermere, circa AD90, (it was once thought to have been built by Agricola in AD79) but was replaced by a larger and more substantial stone structure (approximately 100 metres x 150 metres) circa AD 122, at the time that Hadrian was consolidating Roman influence in the north. The fort was occupied by a cohort of 500 troops until the end of the 4th century when the Roman occupation of the northernmost parts of Britain ended. There have been a number of excavations over the years, most of which have been filled in to preserve the fabric of the site. However a number of interesting features remain on view to the public and have been clearly signed by the National Trust, who purchased Borrans Field by public subscription for £4,000 in 1912. English Heritage are involved with the site, in their role as custodians of Ancient Monuments.

Gummers How is a famous viewpoint opposite Lakeside, about 1 mile up Fell Foot Brow. Approximately 1000 ft in height it commands marvellous views in every direction. The view north takes in the full length of Windermere, whilst if you look south you can follow the River Leven to the sea and Morecambe Bay. Look west to Black Combe, Coniston, Wetherlam, the Langdales, Helvellyn and Fairfield at the lake head, then the Kirkstone Gap, Kentmere and east to Ingleborough and the Pennines, with the Kent Estuary and the far side of Morecambe Bay. Look down to the steamers at Lakeside and the steam trains from Haverthwaite. The effort to attain this viewpoint is well rewarded.

High Dam:- See Stott Park- Bobbin Mill

Hill Top. Beatrix Potter wrote many of her famous stories for children at this 17th- century cottage which she bought in 1905. It contains her personal furniture and china, and is featured in illustrations in many of her books. The "new room" where she did much of her work was restored in 1986. When she died in 1944, by then Mrs Heelis, she left about half of the village of Near Sawrey, 201 acres in all, to the National Trust, including Hill Top, Castle Farm, nine cottages and the Tower Bank Estate.

Lakeside - Haverthwaite Railway. In 1866 the Furness Railway obtained an Act of Parliament to open a link line from Ulverston to Newby Bridge. This was constructed and extended to Lakeside in 1869. Three years later they took over the steamboat company and the rail/steamer link flourished. In 1923 the Furness Railway was acquired by the London, Midland & Scottish Railway (LMS) until Nationalisation in 1947, when it became British Railways. Dr Beeching closed the branch line in 1965. The Lakeside to Haverthwaite section was re-opened by the Lakeside and Haverthwaite Railway Co. Ltd in 1973 and is supported by volunteers of the Lakeside Railway Society.

Lakeside Station was constructed in 1870 for the Furness Railway Co. at a cost of £4461. The first paddle steamer launched at Newby Bridge in 1845 had experienced difficulties when the River Leven was at a low level, no doubt causing the railway company to revise their original plan and extend the line beyond Newby Bridge to the lake shore - Lakeside, thus providing the train/steamer link to the Lakes.

Millerground Cottage was built in 1612, close by a long vanished cornmill, where Wynlass Beck enters the lake. For many years it was the eastern terminus of a passenger ferry, known as "the little boat", crossing to the western shore at Belle Grange where a track led, via Claife Heights, to Hawkshead. The cottage incorporates a belfry that probably housed a bell used to summon the ferry from the opposite shore. Owned by the National Trust since 1913 the cottage is occupied by a private tenant and is not open to the public.

Orrest Head derives its name from the ancient Norse "Orrosta" meaning a battle. Owned by Windermere Town Council it was given in memory of Arthur Henry Heywood of Elleray in 1902. The view from the summit reveals breathtaking views of Windermere in all directions.

Post Knott is owned by the National Trust and is reached by way of a footpath (walk 13) from Bowness. The path was a favourite with Victorian holidaymakers providing easy access to the summit and superb views of Bowness Bay.

Queen Adelaide's Hill is a glacial mound or "drumlin" which rises 130 ft above the lakeshore, named to mark the occasion of Queen Adelaide's visit in 1840. A plaque marks the landing place of the royal party (see walk 10) which reads:- "Queen Adelaide and Suite Landed Here July 26th 1840 and ascended Rayrigg Bank Attended by the Revd. Fletcher and Mrs Fleming". The hill, together with Low Millerground Cottage and boat landings were acquired by the National Trust in 1913, for £5,000, raised by public subscription.

Rawlinson Nab is part of the Graythwaite Estate but since 1969 has been managed by the Lake District National Park Authority. It provides ideal picnic area and public beach access.

Rydal Hall was built by the first Sir Michael Le Fleming in the 16th century and enlarged and altered over the following years. A grade 2 listed building, the hall occupies a magnificent landscape setting next to crashing waterfalls and open parklands. In its time the house has been a family home and hotel and is now a Diocesan Conference and Retreat Centre. The award winning formal gardens, constructed by Thomas Mawson circa 1909, are being restored and are open to the public; there are terraces, lawns, a fountain, flower beds, bridges and a summer house. The old Packhorse route from Ambleside skirts the house and an off road footpath threads its way through Rydal Park to Ambleside.

Rydal Mount and Gardens, "most beloved home" of William Wordsworth who rented it from the Le Fleming family of Rydal Hall from 1813 until his death in 1850. The house now belongs to descendants of the poet and retains a lived-in atmosphere and contains portraits, personal possessions and first editions of his books. The gardens, which he landscaped himself, consist of gentle paths along hillside terraces with rare shrubs and seasonal flowers.

School Knott is situated on Applethwaite Common overlooking Windermere Village, the viewpoint and tarn being privately owned with public access over well defined footpaths. Ancient records refer to Scale Knott and "Scale" is of viking origin meaning "shieling" or "summer grazing ground".

Skelghyll Woods are owned and maintained by the National Trust. There are a number of nature trails through the woods which are particularly attractive in the spring when wild daffodils grow in profusion.

Stock Ghyll, which historically powered corn, bark, fulling and bobbin mills, rises on Red Screes and flows through Stock Ghyll Park to join the River Rothay at Ambleside. Stock Ghyll Force is a waterfall seventy foot high which descends in 2 steps, ideally viewed from the footbridge in Stock Ghyll Park which is owned by South Lakeland District Council.

Stott Park Bobbin Mill was built in 1835 and produced bobbins for the cotton and weaving industry of Lancashire. The versatile lathes, powered by a water supply from **High Dam**, were later used to produce all kinds of wooden objects, enabling it to remain in commercial production until 1971. It is now preserved by English Heritage as a working museum, where the visitor may step back in time to experience at first hand the conditions in which the bobbin makers worked (see photo Page 5).

Town End, Troutbeck is a "statesman" (wealthy yeoman) farmer's house, containing carved woodwork, books, papers, and furniture collected by the Browne family who lived there until 1944. Built by George Browne circa 1626, it has been faithfully restored. Still without electric light, it is tucked into the hillside and displays the distinctive round Westmorland chimneys typical of the area. The house was acquired by the National Trust in 1948 together with the estate of some 776 acres of farmland having been accepted by H. M. Treasury in lieu of death duties.

West's Station was built to provide visitors with their first glimpse of Windermere. West's "Guide to the Lakes in Cumberland, Westmorland and Lancashire" was published in 1778 and in it the author promises that the lakes would provide views "no less surprising than the Alps". He described views obtained from selected "stations", of which the one at the foot of Claife Heights was the first.

Wray Castle is a mock castle owned by the National Trust and built between 1840-47 for Dr. James Dawson of Liverpool in the style of a medieval fortress. The Castle is situated on the slopes of Watbarrow Point and was once a holiday home to Beatrix Potter. It is not open to the public, but you are welcome to walk around the outside, admire the views and examine the many fine trees. The north side faces Ambleside. If you go to the south side you will see the giant conifers and sequoias (redwoods) and if you look carefully a mulberry with a brass plaque inscribed as follows:- This Mulberry Tree Was Planted at The Wray Windermere By William Wordsworth Poet Laureate On the 3rd September 1845.